GET REAL

UNDERSTAND REAL ESTATE
BEFORE IT'S TOO LATE

D1523432

FLIP ROBISON &
DANI LYNN ROBISON

FIRST EDITION

Designed by Biga

First Printing 2023

Flip Robison & Dani Lynn Robison

Freedom Family Publishing

10 9 8 7 6 5 4 3 2 1

GET REAL

Acknowledgements

We would like to thank the following people for their help with this book:

To Abhi Golhar for his resources and feedback as this book began to take life and Matthew Blunt for suggesting the title.

To all of our business and real estate mentors to whom we will always be grateful for leading the way and continuing to be such a big part of our lives to this day.

To our dear family and friends, thank you for always supporting us in all our endeavors. Your unwavering love and encouragement have been our rock and we are grateful for everything you've done for us.

We also want to extend our heartfelt appreciation to all the real estate investors we've worked with over the years. Each deal we've closed taught us something new and valuable, and we couldn't have come this far without your support and collaboration.

To our fellow business owners and entrepreneurs, thank you for being part of our journey and for sharing your knowledge and experiences. The mastermind sessions we've had with you all have been instrumental in shaping our growth and success.

And last but definitely not least, we want to express our deep gratitude to our Freedom Family - our team members and investors spread across the US and the globe. You all have inspired us with your unwavering dedication, hard work, and support, and have made this journey an extraordinary one filled with love, joy, and fulfillment.

Thank you all for being a part of our journey, for inspiring us to push ourselves to greater heights, and for making all our successes possible.

With deep gratitude,

Flip Robison & Dani Lynn Robison

Table of Contents

Acknowledgements   v

High Net Worth Investors' #1 Challenge   11

Real Estate Market Cycle   15

Flip & Dani's Top 5 Investment Strategies   21

Win For Your Family in a Massive Way   61

Find Your Freedom   81

Free Audiobook   87

Chapter 1

High Net Worth Investors' #1 Challenge

For many investors who are just starting out, the biggest hurdle is money.

For high net worth investors who are just starting out, the biggest hurdle is time.

Many of the investors we talk to everyday know how to make money. What they don't know is what to do with their money and how to grow their portfolio in a way that is reliable, secure, and doable in the time that they have to devote to their financial management.

Many of the high net worth individuals we work with are what you might call bootstrappers. They are used to doing their own research and figuring things out on their own. When it comes to money management, they are often not the products of generational wealth. They didn't grow up with family money to fall back on and they want to make sure that they're making good decisions about the money they've earned.

As you'll find out later in the book, that describes us, as well. We've worked hard for our money and we've worked hard for the knowledge that we're sharing with you here. We've built our investment business from the ground up and started all of our companies ourselves. Everything we've done has been born out of necessity, and out of a desire to do things the right way.

Many times, we talk to investors who have tried other investment strategies, only to come to us after having made a number of mistakes during their journey. There's no shame in making mistakes, and when you're working hard to earn that money while also trying to grow it and preserve it for the future, you're bound to make some mistakes.

The first thing most people do with their money is save it. After all, when you're starting out, you're often looking for security above everything else. Of course, the problem with a savings account or other low-risk, low-yield account designed primarily for savings is that you won't get any growth from it.

Next, people move on to something that they think of as the standard way to grow and preserve wealth in this country: stocks and bonds. They may start out with index funds and, if they take an interest in the market, may explore some individual stocks. In fact, it can be fun to buy some shares of a favorite stock like Tesla or Apple. It makes you feel like Daddy Warbucks and gives you bragging rights when you get your new car or iPhone.

Often, however, the growth is slow or, in some cases, market downturns can be difficult to weather. While people say to "buy and hold" for the long term, it's pretty hard to sit and watch the value of your portfolio go down day after day and not be tempted to intervene or sell off things that you know are not going to come back up.

More recently, many people have been swept up into the crypto madness that has swept the investment community, taking advice from YouTube and TikTok and going all-in, believing that crypto and the metaverse offered a whole new world of economic opportunity. For many, that world was just smoke and mirrors and billions if not trillions of dollars have gone up in smoke in just the last few months while the so-called experts have moved on to the next speculative financial instrument.

Finally, some people get interested in real estate investment. It feels like a relief because it's real (as the name implies) and they understand how essential a part of the market it is. In many cases, they may listen to podcasts like ours or explore opportunities by looking for houses in their neighborhood on Zillow or Redfin, but the logistics of property management and the uncertainty of securing a sufficient return on investment may keep them from pursuing real estate as a significant part of their financial growth strategy.

We're here to help. If you've picked up this book, it's because you've gotten turned on to the potential of real estate. However, you're probably just being held back by the logistics.

You know that saying "the devil is in the details"?

That's kind of the situation here. Fortunately, we're here to make the details completely plain and understandable, so that you can create and move forward with a real estate investment strategy that makes sense for you, for your budget, and for the time commitment you have to contribute.

We're going to share our favorite tried-and-true, real-world-tested investment strategies with you so that you can start thinking in a realistic way about real estate investing. We want to demystify the process so that you can enjoy the benefits and opportunities that a well-developed real estate investment strategy can provide.

Now, we believe in being honest and upfront with everyone, so we're not going to pretend we're just sharing this information with you out of the kindness of our hearts. The fact is, we'd love to be able to work with you, as well.

What we've learned is that when people learn about real estate investing, hear how it's worked for us, and develop a strategy that makes sense for them, there are often places where we can plug in and work together. Do you need a friend in the business? We want to be that friend when you're ready and the time is right.

Okay, now that we're all on the same page, let's move forward and talk about how the real estate market works and how high net worth individuals just like you can plug into multiple points in the real estate market cycle to find incredible opportunities.

Chapter 2

Real Estate Market Cycle

You no doubt have a good sense of the basic law of supply and demand. The real estate market follows this same law, with fluctuations in inventory and variations in lifestyles and demographics affecting both the supply of homes and the demand for homes.

Since everybody needs a place to live, why would there be changes in inventory or changes in demand? After all, the population continues to increase in fairly predictable patterns. Isn't there an endlessly increasing demand for real estate investors and professionals to exploit?

Well, yes and no. While some aspects of the real estate cycle are very predictable (and we'll get to those shortly) there are other things that can change. Consider the following scenarios:

- The **2008 mortgage crisis** precipitated years of **foreclosures** and **depressed home values**, affecting both communities and altering the ability of homeowners to qualify for mortgages.

- Prior to the **pandemic in Spring of 2020**, in-town **neighborhoods** and homes on **major commuter routes** were in high demand. After the pandemic, much of that demand shifted to the **outer suburbs** and even to **rural communities** as buyers sought more privacy and outdoor space and began working from home.

Throughout the 2000s, predictable patterns of home sales have been upended by **demographic shifts**, higher levels of **student debt**, rising preferences for **travel** and **entrepreneurship**, and later decision-making regarding **marriage** and **child-bearing**.

All of these large macroeconomic patterns and events resulted in unforeseen impacts on the housing market. Yet the difference between real estate investing and other types of investing is that each also brings its own opportunity.

As one community is impacted negatively, another is impacted positively. As some choose not to buy, opportunities increase for those who own rental properties. Even when the bottom drops out of the market, those who are properly prepared are able to double-down and take advantage of unprecedented opportunities that can set them up for even more long-term gains.

The good news of real estate investing isn't that the market never changes. It's that no matter how the market changes, there is a rational response that savvy investors can use to continue to grow their portfolio.

Now let's look at the four parts of the real estate market cycle and the opportunities each offers:

Recession

You're probably familiar with the broad outlines of an economic recession, when the economy retracts for two consecutive quarters. In most cases, this is accompanied by huge corrections and losses in the stock market and contractions in spending and in the economy at large.

For real estate investors, the opportunity available during a recession is unparalleled. Short sales and pre-foreclosure properties go on the market and offer the chance to buy at a deep discount. If an investor has solid connections in the real estate community or if you have a marketing outreach plan in place, they should be able to find many off-market and pre-market deals.

For those who are looking to finance deals without ongoing property ownership or management, the proliferation of deals means that there will be many opportunities for private money lending to other investors, whether they're flipping or buying and holding.

Recovery

As the recession comes to an end, the recovery phase will continue to offer a host of prime opportunities for jumping into the real estate investing landscape. There will still be plenty of deals to be had, but with a recovery, there is also more upside to be obtained, so there are sellers as well as buyers participating in the market.

That means that when an investor finds a great deal, they have more options to choose from. They may decide to:

- Wholesale that deal to another investor

- Rehab the property and add additional value for either a subsequent sale (flipping) or to increase its rental rate

- Buy and hold the property long term as part of a rental portfolio

- Fund acquisitions and rehabs as a private money lender

Expansion

During the expansion phase of the real estate cycle, an investor will still be able to find deals and, when they're shopping smart, they can still add enough value to flip a property and experience significant profit potential. This is especially true as some communities will experience new growth or rehabilitation during an expansion phase, resulting in overall higher home values in that market.

Similarly, buy and hold investments in new or growing areas can be particularly profitable. It may be worth it to make some updates and upgrades to investments in these areas, especially if they are becoming more upscale. This may allow you to charge higher rental rates and experience greater profitability overall on your investment.

Here too, connections in the commercial real estate community are invaluable as they can help predict where new commercial development will take place. This can often be a predictor for new jobs and new amenities that will result in new residential construction and development.

Hyper-supply

During the hyper-supply phase, there is significant inventory to go around, leading to less demand. Often this occurs as an over-response to the expansion phase, or too much new inventory in a particular niche. For example, in some markets, overbuilding in condos or luxury homes has led to a hyper-supply in those market segments, though not in the broader inventory.

During the hyper-supply phase, the market is looking for its balance, so home values may still be high based on the previous expansion phase, even as demand is slowing. In many cases, investors are paying more for properties, so buy and hold is generally the preferred way to monetize these properties.

Later, if desired, there may be an opportunity to exit some of the properties in the portfolio, but an initial buy and hold phase is preferable to optimize value.

Along with the effect on the acquisition of properties

and the strategies used to monetize them, these phases will have an effect on the rental market. Investors employing a buy and hold strategy will need to be aware of the level of vacancies and the competition for rental properties in their market.

Chapter 3

Flip & Dani's Top 5 Investment Strategies

Later in this book, we'll talk about our own personal experiences with real estate investment. While we've done a lot of different types of deals and made use of plenty of different strategies, we haven't done everything. We're not here to tell you about every possible real estate investment strategy out there.

We strongly believe in boots-on-the-ground experience when it comes to sharing our expertise, whether that's through coaching, advising, consulting, partnering, or, as in this case, educating through content. We don't want to tell you about strategies that we haven't tested for ourselves and that we can't vouch for.

For that reason, we've put together a list of our favorite strategies here—those that are tried and true and dependable. The advantage of having multiple strategies goes back to what we talked about in the last chapter: As the market changes, having more than one way to enter or exit the market gives you options so that you can always invest and always find areas of potential and profitability.

Strategy 1: Private Money Lending

For high net worth individuals who are just starting out in real estate investing, this is probably the easiest way into real estate investing. It has the lowest barrier to entry because all it really requires is what you have—money to invest—and someone to partner with who has a track record of success and expertise.

The objective of lending, of course, is to lend capital to qualified borrowers for a return on investment. That return can come in the form of the interest you charge as well as fees and other charges associated with the loan itself.

The private part of private lending is what you may be wondering about. After all, if these borrowers are a good risk, why don't they just head on over to the bank or talk to their friendly neighborhood mortgage officer, right? Well, there are a variety of reasons an investor might prefer to work with a private money lender. These include:

Speed: Time is of the essence when you're making deals, and the time it takes to get a traditional loan can make it impossible to get deals done in a timely manner.

Cash or cash-equivalent capability: To get the best deals, you often need to come in with an all-cash offer or the equivalent—an immediately fundable offer that's as good as cash. Traditional financing won't do for this kind of deal.

Flexibility: Sometimes you have multiple deals going

on at once. Sometimes you need to fund an acquisition and rehab at the same time. Traditional mortgage products are not set up with the flexibility needed for many of the real-world scenarios investors commonly face.

For these and many other reasons, sources of timely and dependable funding are always in demand. Thus, private money lending can be a great way for you to get your feet wet in the world of investing, by working with experienced investors without having to do the dirty work of finding and managing properties yourself.

The best part, of course, is that unlike pouring money into the stock market, the funds you provide to a well-qualified real estate investor are backed by the collateral value of the property itself. If the investor's deal goes sour, you'll get your money out of the deal by taking possession of and monetizing the property itself.

Determining creditworthiness: The 5 C's

How do you know that an investor you're interested in working with is really on the up and up? After all, banks have an exhaustive process for determining who is creditworthy. How can you duplicate that process as a private lender?

First of all, we definitely suggest that you protect yourself with the appropriate legal advice and documentation so that you and your money are properly collateralized in the deal. You should also do your due diligence to make sure the deal is everything it appears to be during the investor's pitch.

However, we've found that the 5 C's are a great indicator of the creditworthiness of a borrower. Make sure you go through these to determine whether the investor you're considering is worthy of your trust and time.

Character: Character speaks to the kind of person the investor is. Are they trustworthy? Do they pay their debts? Some objective measures of character include credit score and credit history as well as past performance in handling debt obligations.

Capacity: Capacity measures the level of cash flow and the ability to repay the debt. You'll want to ensure that the subject property is properly valued so that you can feel confident it will pay you back in the event of a default by the borrower.

Capital: Capital involves looking at the borrower's level of debt, net worth and equity to gauge their access to capital, and thus, their ability to pay. This is one reason that lenders rarely provide 100 percent of the funding for a deal—you want the borrower to have skin in the game and at least some cash on hand.

Conditions: This is where you look at the proposed project itself. Where is the property? What improvements does the investor have in mind? How do they intend to use the money you're loaning them? It's important to make sure that their planning is realistic (and that they have a plan in place).

Collateral: For real estate investing, collateral—or the asset(s) pledged to back the loan—will be the property itself. Make sure you have an exit strategy in place so that you can get your money out of the property if necessary.

The best part of private money lending is that, once you have a reliable process in place and a team of advisors, you will never lack for deals. In fact, you will probably find that soon you will have a group of seasoned, experienced investors who will want to work with you—and with whom you'll want to work — again and again in the years to come for reliable returns.

Strategy 2: Single Family Rentals (SFR)

When you think about real estate investing, you probably think about single family rentals or SFR. In fact, building a portfolio of single family rentals is the goal for many real estate investors, either in the short-term or long-term.

Why is this such a popular asset class for real estate investors? For most, the objective is to build long-term wealth, and virtually nothing does that as reliably as single family rentals. That's because individual homes last for decades and, barring major negative changes in the condition of the home or its surrounding community, rise in value during those decades.

In addition, single family rentals offer tax benefits when passed along to your heirs, and may allow them to inherit a well-managed property portfolio at a significant tax savings. (*As always, check with your tax advisor for the latest rules regarding inheritance and income taxes.*)

In addition, at least in our experience, one of the benefits of SFR's is their familiarity. We all know what a well-maintained house looks like. We all understand the kind of basic maintenance it takes to keep it up properly and preserve its value.

Whether you live in a mansion or a bungalow at the beach, you understand the fundamentals of buying and holding a home and taking care of it long term. That is half the battle when it comes to SFR investing.

The other half of the battle is where people get hung up, and that's property management or, more specifically, tenant management. You may be concerned about marketing the property and keeping it filled with well-qualified tenants who pay on time and take care of the place.

Almost every real estate investor has horror stories about bad tenants or about downturns where a property sat vacant for a few months and ate into their cash reserves. For this reason, we are always clear when we suggest professional property management to our coaching and consulting clients. They can take care of both the maintenance and tenant-relations headaches, making SFR ownership far more doable and, ultimately, profitable.

How to evaluate an SFR

Determining whether a single family rental property

is a good investment often starts with evaluating its market. While the home itself generally needs to be in solid condition, you can make changes and improvements to the structure and the landscaping—what you can't change is the location.

Here are some questions to consider when looking at the market for your SFR:

Is the local economy strong?

Remember the people who are likely to be renting a single-family home: Middle-class families looking for workforce housing with jobs in manufacturing, distribution, logistics, education, public health, medical facilities, local government and public service.

Does the local housing market show stable appreciation over the past several years?

Look for good rent ratios and positive cash flow potential. Remember, you always want to have an exit strategy in order to multiply your potential return on investment and to protect your capital should the market or your investment strategy shift.

Is there an appropriate balance of supply and demand?

There should be a balanced market between rental demand and available inventory. There should also be a balance between owned properties and rented properties in the area.

Does the area have a selection of quality properties available at any given time?

Depending on your investment strategy, you may be looking for class A new construction homes with upgraded finishes to minimize future maintenance expenses. Alternatively, you may be looking for well-built, solid homes with acceptable fixtures and finishes but without all of the bells and whistles available in newer homes. It's important to have a good understanding of the norms for the market you're serving.

What is the quality of the neighborhoods around the property you're considering?

Ideally, you'd like to see a preponderance of owner-occupied homes occupied by working families who are likely to remain in place long-term. In addition, quality school districts are often major determinants for renters. Look for communities where the average home price is slightly above the median price point for the local area.

Are rents high enough in the area to provide adequate ROI and cash flow?

You're looking for a rent ratio of approximately 1%. This is calculated by dividing the monthly rent by the value of the property.

Are taxes and insurance rates low and affordable?

Here you're looking for property tax rates between 0.6 percent and 1.6 percent with modestly priced landlord insurance.

Is the legal environment favorable for landlords?

A landlord friendly state and municipality is a must to

protect yourself and the value of your investment long-term.

5 tips for successful SFR investing

Of course, you'll learn many small strategies during your time as a single family real estate investor, but when you're first starting out, here are the five essentials that you need to know to maximize your chances for success:

1. Determine how you will finance your property and ensure that you have an adequate cash reserve.

For many high net worth individuals, cash is king when it comes to investing. However, you may want to retain at least a portion of your available cash or avoid having all of your equity tied up at once in an investment property.

Determining how you will structure your investment and how you will finance the non-cash portion is essential to ensure that you're maintaining a solid ROI and that you're growing at the pace you want over time. In addition, you'll need to make sure you have adequate access to cash in case of vacancies or needed repairs to the property.

2. Understand rental property returns and run the numbers up front.

To understand your return on investment, you'll need to know your costs for acquisition, preparing the property for market, carrying costs, property management, taxes, and many other associated expenses.

This is no time to "wing it" and assume everything will work out on the balance sheet at the end of the year. Make sure you are running numbers up front and getting a solid sense of your potential return on investment before you take the plunge into a property.

3. Find a rental property that meets the criteria you have pre-determined for success.

Once you've put your numbers together and started shopping, it's easy to fall in love with a property and imagine that it offers a reason to deviate from the plan you've laid out. This is a mistake, especially when you're first starting out.

Once you've been investing for a while and have a variety of experiences under your belt, you may be able to take your gut instinct into account when looking at properties. Up front, however, you need to make sure that you're sticking to your predetermined plan to ensure a successful financial outcome.

4. Hire a professional property manager to avoid living the landlord lifestyle.

If you don't mind the idea of someone calling you at 3 a.m. to unclog a toilet, you may want to save the money you'd spend on professional property management and manage your SFR yourself. If, however, like most high net worth individual investors, you'd prefer to farm out that responsibility and hassle, a property manager is essential to your success.

Not only will professional property management keep you from having to make late-night emergency repair calls. They'll also have systems and processes in place for finding tenants, gathering rent payments, and intervening in the event of problems with non-payment or damage to the property.

It bears repeating: unless you're looking for a very time-consuming second job, we strongly recommend professional property management of your SFR portfolio.

5. Track income and expenses on an ongoing basis and revisit your numbers consistently to ensure adequate ongoing ROI.

The property that starts out profitably may begin to lose some of its shine if rental rates stagnate due to increased inventory in the area. A long-term buy and hold strategy may shift if a neighborhood suddenly becomes more desirable and renters are looking for upgraded features.

SFR is not a one-and-done proposition. Make sure you keep revisiting your numbers and your properties on an ongoing basis. The idea is to ensure that you're constantly optimizing their potential value or, in the event of a negative shift, looking for an exit strategy if necessary.

How to analyze a specific SFR deal

When you're looking for a deal, you'll want to create a process to evaluate each potential property. Here's a five-step filter for your individual SFR deals.

Step One: Location, location, location

You know that anything real estate-related will eventually use the number one criterion for real estate deal-making: Location, location, location.

Look at the neighborhood and factor in the same types of items you'd consider if you were looking for a home. These may include things like:

- School performance
- Walkability
- Access to parking or public transportation
- Proximity to attractions, amenities or recreation
- Proximity to shopping and conveniences

Consider the type of renter who'll be looking for a rental in that area. Will it be a family with small children? This is likely if you're looking at a suburban neighborhood. Will it be a young professional couple, perhaps with a pet? This is likely if you're looking at an in-town neighborhood.

Step Two: Crunch the numbers

Next, you're going to look at comparable rental properties in the area. That will help you to understand how much you can expect to bring in each month and help you calculate cash flow and other important numbers.

How do you know what properties are comparable to the one you're considering? Look for:

Proximity: This could mean within three blocks in a small downtown neighborhood or within a few miles in a suburban market.

Size: This includes square footage, but also the numbers of bedrooms and bathrooms, which should be the same.

Lot: This is especially important if the lot is oversized, fenced, or desirably situated.

Amenities: This can become an important factor if you're looking at a home in an HOA neighborhood where there are many resort-style or club-style amenities that could affect value and potential rental rate.

Condition: Is the home distressed, updated, or otherwise in the same condition as the house you are looking at?

Days on Market: Try to avoid choosing homes that have been sitting on the market for longer than 60 days. They may have a problem that you're not aware of and may reflect a lower rental rate because of it.

Step Three: Calculate an estimated rent rate

Determine an estimated rent rate by dividing the monthly rent by the square footage of the comps you've chosen. Then apply the resulting rate per square foot to the home you're looking at. Be sure to differentiate if your home is in better condition or has amenities that the comps do not reflect.

Remember, if there is a pool, spacious yard, or other upgraded fixtures or finishes, you should differentiate the rent rate, especially if you will also be providing extra maintenance for any of these features.

Step Four: Adjust the rent rate as needed

Take into account additional factors that might determine rent rate. Do you need to account for occupancy rate in your market? Will you be providing lawn care or requiring the renter to provide it? Do you anticipate the need for major repairs or systems replacement in the next few years? Do you want to differentiate according to the length of the lease terms? This is the time to tweak your initial estimate and come up with a more solid rent rate that you'll advertise for your rental property.

Step Five: Determine how much you'll pay for the property

Once you've made up your mind that you've found the right property, it's time to work backwards from the projected rent rate and calculate the acquisition and carrying costs for the property. The idea is to generate solid cash on cash return and profit.

Because you'll probably be negotiating for a lower-than-asking purchase price, it's helpful to work with someone who can help you locate pre-market or off-market properties that fit your investment criteria. These sellers are more likely to be flexible and willing to negotiate than those who have listed their homes on the MLS and are locked into an idea of its fair market value.

Strategy 3: Flipping

For those who are seeking the ability to generate significant income in a shorter period of time, without the ongoing management responsibility of buy and hold SFR, flipping may be a preferred option. This short-term investment strategy is probably one that you've seen on HGTV or other DIY-related channels and involves purchasing a property, adding value to it, then selling it at a profit that's sufficient to cover acquisition, rehab, improvement, and carrying costs.

Over the last couple of years, low inventory has been a major problem in markets all over the country, and it is projected to continue to create issues for the foreseeable future. Simply put, for a variety of reasons, from pandemic-related shortages of labor and materials to change in tastes and preferences, there simply aren't enough homes being built for the demand in the market.

That means that the ability to locate off-market properties, add value to them, and get them on the market promises to be a profitable investment strategy for years to come.

How can you tell a good flip from a bad flip?

While you may think that analyzing a house flip is as simple as finding a home that's a bargain and giving it a fresh coat of paint, there's actually a lot more that goes into successfully monetizing a flip. Remember, this is more than putting lipstick on a pig: You want to make sure that the improvements you make are actually adding value in the market where you're selling.

Here are six steps to analyzing a flip:

1. Determine the after repair value, or ARV, for the property you're interested in. This will help you figure out how much you'll be able to sell the property for once all of your changes are complete.

Remember the comps that you pulled in the last section? You'll do something similar here to come up with the ARV. Just make sure you're comparing the home to properties that are comparable to its finished condition once all of your repairs and upgrades have been completed.

2. Drill down on the specific improvements you'll need to make to the property to get to the ARV you've projected in the previous step.

This is where a great home inspector comes into play. You'll want to make sure you have a solid sense of what it will take to get the property market ready, including both the cosmetic bells and whistles and the behind-the-wall systems repairs and replacements you'll need to do.

3. Price out the improvements you've identified to come up with a budget for your flip.

This is where you'll need a reliable contractor to ensure that you have a solid sense of how much everything is going to be. Remember, you need someone who's going to get in there and get the work finished on time and on-budget, because time is of the essence, as you'll see in the next step.

4. Calculate your carrying costs, including financing,

holding costs, taxes, insurance, and fees associated with the transaction.

Every day that you own the home, you are paying for that ownership. In addition, you have to pay the costs associated with acquiring and selling the home. Make sure that you are accurately calculating all of those costs so that you can keep your eye on the bottom line. In addition, as closely as possible, make sure you know how long you'll have to carry the home before you're able to exit and monetize it.

5. Figure out how much profit you'll need to make to make the flip worthwhile.

For some luxury properties, a full-scale renovation of many months may be worthwhile because the profit anticipated could total into the millions. For a small single-family home, you may need to get in and out quickly in order to make enough money to make the flip worth it to you. Calculate not only the costs associated with the process itself, but also the amount of time, travel and attention you'll have to pay to the flip to make it worthwhile to you.

6. Based on the data you've gathered, determine the maximum amount you'd be willing to pay for the property's acquisition.

There's an old (and true) saying in real estate investment: You make your money on the purchase, not the sale. While you may add value with smart upgrades and you may sell for more than you've anticipated, the make or break for most deals is at the time of acquiring the property.

Figure out what is the most you're willing to pay to get that property, then start your negotiations below that. If you're working with a wholesaler, make sure your acquisition cost accounts for the amount you'll have to pay them for finding the property as well.

Terms, concepts and formulas to remember:

Project Costs

Project costs include all of the costs associated with the project from acquisition through closing. Here's a simple formula:

Project Costs = Acquisition or Purchase Price + Fees Costs Associated with the Purchase + Carrying Costs + Rehab and Repair Costs + Costs Associated with the Sale of the Property

Profit

Profit is the amount of money you can expect to clear after the project is complete. Determine what the minimum profit required will be and let that be your guide as you make your decisions.

Profit = After Repair Value (ARV) – Project Costs

Return on Investment (ROI)

This is the ratio of profit to the investment itself.

ROI = Profit / Project Costs

Many real estate investors look for a return on investment of at least 15 percent to 20 percent in order to deem a project worthwhile.

Rate of Return (ROR)

Rate of return is the ROI over a particular period of time, typically a year. Calculate it this way:

$$ROR = ROI/Holding\ Days * 365$$

Remember, even if ROI is higher for one project over another, if the ROR is lower, it may be taking too much time to flip that type of property. Look for an ROR of 30 percent.

Maximum Allowable Offer (MAO)

This is the maximum amount you are willing to pay for the acquisition of a property. It can be calculated using either your projected ROI (preferably 15 percent to 20 percent for many flippers) or the 70 percent rule.

70 Percent Rule

Until you really know your numbers, the 70 percent rule allows you to develop a fair estimate of what you'll need to make a deal work. The formula is:

$$MAO = (ARV * 70\%) - Rehab\ Costs$$

Days on Market

One of the things you'll want to know when you're calculating carrying costs is the average days on market for homes in the area. That will give you an idea of how long it will take to sell the home once the work has been completed. This number should be added in as you calculate your total project costs.

Absorption Rate

Similarly, absorption rate helps you figure out how much demand there is in an area and may be a useful metric to consider as you're determining whether a deal is worth pursuing. It lets you know how many people are buying in the area where your subject property is located and whether it's a seller's market, buyer's market, or a balanced market that's somewhere between the two.

Absorption Rate (in Days) = Active Listings * Time Period / Sold Listings in Time Period

An **absorption rate** of:

Based on a 30 day time period the absorption rate equals the number of homes sold divided by the number of available homes.

20 % and greater is a **seller's market**

15 % and lower is a **buyers market**

Calculating a deal: EXAMPLE

Imagine you're looking at a 1500 square foot, three bedroom, two bath property in a medium demand neighborhood. You've looked at the comps and the **ARV for the property is $175,000**. The seller is asking **$100,000** for the property.

The home needs quite a bit of exterior work, including:

- A new roof
- New windows
- Exterior paint

The interior needs:

- Remodeled kitchen and bath
- New fixtures and finishes throughout

While you're waiting for a detailed estimate from your contractor, you can plug in a rough estimate for the proposed repairs. These generally run $30 to $50 per square foot. Assuming an average on the low side of $35 per square foot in this case, we've **projected repair costs of $52,000**.

Buying costs are generally around one percent to three percent of the purchase price, so on a $100,000 purchase, assuming two percent, that's **$2000**.

Assuming you're paying cash, there are no financing costs. Let's assume **carrying costs** of **$750** for five months to cover utilities, property taxes and insurance.

Selling costs are generally six percent to nine percent for this market, so assume eight percent in this case, times the ARV or $175,000. That equals **$14,000**.

Next, how much **profit** do you need to make on the deal? If you're assuming 15 percent, that would be **$26,000** based on the ARV of $175,000.

Now, remember the seller's desired purchase price of $100,000? Based on our numbers, we'd only be making $2,700 on this flip at that pur-

chase price. In order to get to the $26,000 we're expecting in profit, **you'd need to offer no more than $76,000.**

See how important it is to start with the profit you need, then work backward? Otherwise, you could look at that $75,000 difference between the asking price and the ARV and assume there'll be plenty of room in there to cover your profit. It's just not necessarily so.

Many investors fall in love with flipping because it gives you the chance for big rewards and there's always something new to do. If you think flipping might be the right strategy for you, just make sure you know your numbers and put them to work on every deal.

Strategy 4: Self-Storage

There's no doubt about it: People love **STUFF**, and they are unwilling to part with it. That makes the self-storage segment of real estate investment a consistently growing one, and it is the reason that it's one of our favorite strategies.

According to a 2022 report by Marcus and Millichap, self-storage as an investment vehicle makes sense, especially right now, for a couple of different reasons:

1. The health crisis brought about by the effects of the pandemic drove unprecedented demand for these units, while labor and material shortages kept new ones from being built. That has meant fresh capital coming into existing properties without diluting the sector through oversupply.

2. The fact that self-storage units are rented on a month-to-month basis makes self-storage one of the strongest types of real estate investment categories for responding quickly to changing market conditions. That makes this sector one of the strongest inflation hedge options among the other categories of real estate investment types.

In addition, the low inventory residential housing market has driven an increase in demand for self-storage units. As many hopeful buyers have had to put off upsizing into larger homes, the solution has become storing items and furniture in self-storage units instead. One interesting feature of self-storage units is the ease with which they can be updated and upgraded, providing investors with the opportunity to add value. For example, as younger users and post-pandemic consumers have become more accustomed to online reservation and check-in options, adding online portals offer a cost-effective way to increase the perceived value of a self-storage facility for minimal cost.

By the numbers: What makes self-storage such a good investment option?

Self-storage offers a host of benefits for investors, especially those looking for a more passive investment opportunity. Here are just a few of the ways that self-storage provides superior ROI when compared to some other categories of real estate investment.

Superior cashflow: Compare the cost of maintaining a self-storage facility at 90 percent occupancy to the cost of maintaining a single-family residence or a multi-family residential community. Forget clogged toilets in the middle of the night or tenants who don't mow the lawn. The simple logistics of maintaining a self-storage facility, and the relatively fixed state of most of the occupancy, makes this a simpler and much more profitable type of real estate investment than most others.

According to some industry analysts, positive cash on cash ROI for self-storage facilities has typically averaged nearly 30 percent. That adds up to a buy and hold strategy with maximum cash flow and minimal management: a true win-win.

Lower cost of development: The cost of development for a self-storage facility is primarily based on both the cost of suitable land and the cost of building the structures themselves. If you are considering developing a ground-up self-storage facility, site work and utilities will be the biggest variables. Materials themselves are fairly fixed, unlike residential real estate development where fixtures and finishes can make an enormous difference in the final cost of construction.

More reliable financial projections: On average, many self-storage owner-operators find that they can break even with occupancy levels as low as 60 percent to 72 percent, depending on their market and their financing. This offers a great deal of leeway for profitability, especially in high-demand markets where occupancy levels may hover at or near 100 percent.

Keep in mind, 100 percent occupancy is not the goal with self-storage. If a facility is operating at 100 percent occupancy, it often indicates that rental rates are too low for the area.

Greater rate of success: According to a study of commercial real estate investment sectors, the rate of failure reported during an economic recession was:

- Multifamily = failure rate of 58 percent
- Office = failure rate of 63 percent
- Retail = failure rate of 53 percent
- Self storage = failure rate of 8 percent

Thus, even during negative conditions in the broader economy, self-storage as an investment sector tends to thrive, in part as a haven for those who have lost offices, storefronts, and other commercial facilities.

Self-storage market fundamentals: During good economic times, when businesses are scaling up, commercial tenants turn to self-storage for extra warehouse space to offer them greater flexibility in meeting customer demand.

During bad economic times, residential customers begin downsizing, resulting in a need for self-storage as a place to leave additional furniture and mementos that won't fit into smaller living spaces.

Regardless of conditions in the broader macroeconomic environment, there is upside potential for self-storage facilities and investors.

Self-storage rental fundamentals: Self-storage rental costs per square foot are similar to those for multifamily residential units. However, development and management costs are one-third to one-half as much. This built-in profit margin is a major aspect of the appeal of self-storage as a long-term investment category.

What to look for in a potential self-storage facility

Besides the nuts and bolts, and dollars and cents, of the self-storage facility, there are some considerations to take into account that you'll be familiar with from residential real estate investing. These include:

Classification: There are three facility classes, A, B, and C, just as you'll find with other types of commercial real estate investment. Classification of the self-storage facility is driven by the quality of construction, location and access, management and security, and high-end amenities, for example, climate-controlled units. Classification will affect cost, maintenance, and marketability of your self-storage facility.

Condition: Here you'll want to look at the condition of the doors, the asphalt and other hardscapes, the office or common areas, and the HVAC units, if it's a climate-controlled facility. Look for water or fire damage or any indication of deferred maintenance as well.

In addition, consider sources of liability under environmental laws, plus the presence of asbestos, toxic mold, petroleum products, lead-based paint and so on. Your lender may require an Environmental Site Assessment as well.

Security: Find out what kind of security is in place at the facility currently, both personnel and infrastructure. This may include cameras, alarms, perimeter fencing, barrier arms, gates, locks and the fire protection system.

Size: Make sure that the facility is large enough to spread out fixed costs such as management and maintenance. In many cases, that will mean having more than 50,000 square feet of leasable area. In addition, if you're planning to provide 24-hour on-site management, you may need an on-site office and apartment.

Zoning: Make sure that the existing facility complies with local zoning laws and ordinances. If you are developing a new facility, work with your real estate professional or real estate attorney to ensure compliance. For developers, a requirement to hold public hearings before approval is one of the biggest barriers to the development of new self-storage facilities. Consider working with a marketing or PR professional to position your project positively.

Aesthetics and visibility: Consider the benefits of landscaping, lighting, and other elements to make your facility as attractive as possible. Not only will it make it acceptable to zoning officials and interest groups, but it will help to market the property and make it more attractive to potential customers. Make sure signage, entrances, and exits all enjoy ample visibility 24 hours a day.

How to analyze a self-storage deal

Ready to look at the numbers on a self-storage facility? Here's where to start:

1. Confirm unit rents

Start by looking at current unit rents for each type of unit in the self-storage facility. In addition, look at comps for similar self-storage facilities in the area and confirm rents for those with value-added upgrades you may be considering, including security features or climate control.

2. Confirm operating costs

Determine how much it costs to staff and maintain the self-storage facility, as well as whatever additional services you might be providing. For example, if you're adding on-site management where it has not existed before, you'll need to factor in those costs.

Some standard costs may include:

- Security system fees (automated and/or in-person)
- Utilities
- Custodial fees
- Marketing fees
- Property taxes
- Insurance
- Maintenance
- Accounting fees

3. Determine property value

For commercial value, use the following formula:

Property Value = Net Operating Income (NOI) / Capitalization ("Cap") Rate

With smart, low-cost property improvements and related increases in the rental rate, NOI can increase significantly within even the first few months of ownership. That can lower the cap rate and create a more stable, higher quality investment property for the long term.

4. Explore commercial financing opportunities

If you want to keep some of your cash free to explore other investment opportunities, you can explore commercial financing options. For commercial mortgages, most lenders will provide up to 75 percent LTV (loan-to-value), which may allow you to use some of your cash for improvements to the subject property or for additional acquisitions.

5. Confirm budget and financing

This is where you look at the value of the property, the improvements you've decided to make, and the financing option you've chosen to pursue. This will give you a financing scenario so that you can determine what your real numbers will look like and you can begin to put together the details of the deal, including your commercial lender, if required, and your contractor.

6. Project cash flow and investment criteria

Finally, with real numbers in place, you can calculate your IRR (Internal Rate of Return) and find out if the potential investment meets your criteria. Just as with SFRs and flips, if the numbers don't work, you don't want to do the investment.

Strategy 5: Multi-family

Many people think of multi-family investing as inherently more complicated and difficult than SFR. However, as you'll see from our personal experience in the next section, in some regards multi-family can be simpler than maintaining a large portfolio of single family homes.

In addition, the real estate purchase market of the pandemic-era has been very good to the multifamily market. Rising home prices, followed by higher than normal interest rates, have combined to ensure that many tenants are finding it more cost-effective to continue renting, so a well managed, well-maintained multi-family community can pay dividends.

On top of that, multifamily communities provide ample opportunity to add value in a way that is cost-effective and can result in significant ROI for years after the improvements. Even the addition of one or two outdoor amenities can make a significant difference in visibility, marketability, rent rate, and occupancy levels year after year.

According to research by CBRE Group, the world's largest commercial real estate services and investment company, the multifamily sector is experiencing "solid fundamentals and heightened investor interest. With tremendous liquidity and a growing range of debt options available, multifamily pricing will be as strong as ever."

In addition, as the post-pandemic working environment returns to something more like normal, multifamily properties in urban markets are seeing a return to their pre-pandemic level of demand, while those in suburban markets are not experiencing the falloff that might have been expected by a return to the office.

This suggests an overall resurgence in this investment sector and ongoing strength across the board for investors in multifamily properties.

How to analyze a multifamily deal

When you're looking at multifamily deals, you'll find that some of the elements that mattered with SFR apply just as much to multifamily. Here are some things to keep in mind when analyzing a multifamily property.

1. Location, Location, Location

Yes, there it is again, and it may be even more important for multifamily than for single family residential properties. That's because the best multifamily properties often take advantage of proximity to great multiuse or commercial centers or provide workforce housing for large employers. In addition, in college towns or in submarkets with colleges, multi-family properties that are properly managed may enjoy long-term and consistent popularity and competitive rental rates.

Some of the factors to consider when evaluating the location of a multifamily property include:

- School performance (if located in a suburban or exurban market)
- Walkability (especially important in urban markets)
- Access to parking or public transportation
- Proximity to attractions, amenities or recreation
- Proximity to colleges or major employment hubs
- Proximity to shopping and conveniences

2. The job market

Growth in the job market is a major predictor of growth in the multifamily investor segment. The addition of a major employer can mean a huge boon, both for existing multifamily communities and for developers of new communities. Similarly, a shrinking job market or the loss of a major employer can have an outsized impact on multifamily communities.

3. Median income

While you may think of multifamily rentals as a lower priced alternative to the purchase of a single-family home, you still want to ensure that you're investing in an area with medium to high average income demographics. This will provide more reassurance for the long-term health of the market and better ROI potential on your investment.

4. Safety

Safety is often an important consideration for multi-family renters, both while they're on property and while they're accessing local amenities or public transportation. Walkability and proximity to local commercial options are both common reasons for choosing a particular area and a particular multifamily community, so being able to provide reassurance about safety, and providing a reasonable expectation of safety while on property, are important factors for remaining competitive.

5. Market analysis

Of course, this goes back to the idea of location, but it is more nuanced than that. A market analysis will drill down to individual communities and submarkets to find the areas that are most likely to provide significant ROI and generate long-term demand.

Conducting a multi-family deal analysis

Step One: Analyze the purchase price

Here you'll begin by assessing the property value vs. the asking price. As with so many of the other investment property strategies we've discussed, this starts with identifying appropriate comps for the multifamily property you're interested in.

Look for a multifamily property with similar square footage and amenities as the property you're interested in. This can help you determine whether the asking price is realistic or, if not, what would be an appropriate purchase price.

Step Two: Analyze the financial data

Next, you'll calculate the cost of repairs as well as the costs associated with the acquisition of the property. These include closing costs including the appraisal, taxes, attorney's fees, and so on.

In your repair costs, you'll want to include the cost of any improvements you're thinking of making. Make sure that you'll be able to get a sufficient return on investment for improvements and that you don't add costly upgrades or amenities that might price the property out of its market.

Net cost = property price + cost of repairs + closing costs

Next, determine how much income the property can be expected to generate. Include the total of passive income for things like parking facilities, laundry facilities, ancillary services, and other amenities that are priced separately from the base rental rate. In addition, make sure that you've accounted for the fair market rental rate that accounts for the repairs and improvements you're making, especially if the property is currently operating at a below-market rate.

Finally, calculate your projected expenses, including the cost of property management, taxes, insurance, maintenance, landscaping, and utilities. Double check tax assessments for the previous years and make sure there are no upcoming assessments or changes to the tax structure that would materially affect the costs associated with the property.

Step Three: Analyze net operating income

Next, calculate the NOI or Net Operating Income as follows:

Net Operating Income = Income (rent, parking, etc.) – Operating cost (taxes, insurance, management, maintenance, etc.).

Step Four: Analyze cash flow

If you are financing the property, subtract the mortgage payment from the NOI. Taxes and insurance payments may come out in this stage as well. This is not the place to take out variable expenses like utilities and maintenance.

Cash flow = Net Operating Income – Mortgage Payment

Step Five: Analyze Projected ROI (Return on Investment)

If your cash flow projection is positive, it's time to calculate the potential ROI for the property. The formula for this is as follows:

ROI = Cash flow ÷ Investment Cost

(down payment + closing costs + rehab costs)

Just as with the other investment opportunities, you'll need to determine what ROI is appropriate for you. Many seasoned stock market investors view an eight percent return annually to be a reasonable ROI, so you may want to use that as a baseline and look for an ROI that provides 15 percent to 20 percent, allowing you to outpace the stock market.

Step Six: Calculate net ROI

Here you'll continue to look at other benefits, including tax deductions, equity growth, and property appreciation. This will give you a sense of the big picture of how your investment's returns may (or may not) increase over time. A common way to calculate *net ROI = Total Return ÷ Investment Cost*

Strategy 6: Investing in businesses

Called private equity investing, this strategy involves buying and managing companies prior to selling them. It's a little different from most real estate investing, but it's a strategy that we have found to be interesting, enjoyable, and rewarding.

Private equity investors may either buy a business outright or as part of a group of other private equity investors. The idea is to overhaul the business in order to add value before subsequently finding an appropriate buyer.

What is the difference between private equity investing and venture capital?

You may be familiar with venture capitalists who purchase, either in whole or in part, start-up companies and help to fund their growth and expansion. As you can imagine, this can be a risky proposition, especially in emerging markets and emerging industries where no one knows much about the technology or service that's being developed for the first time.

By contrast, private equity is designed for more mature companies, which brings with it a number of advantages:

- Mature businesses often bring with them the expertise and insight of their founders or long-time employees, who may be persuaded to stay and help with day-to-day operations.
- Mature businesses already have the infrastructure, systems, and processes in place, so you're not having to fund these elements of the business.
- Mature businesses already have a client base, market share, and other elements that can be exploited, even if they are undergoing difficulties.
- Mature businesses have assets that make them valuable. The key is figuring out how to take advantage of the elements that are in place, encourage growth where possible, and develop an exit strategy that makes sense.

A successful private equity position may allow you to add value up front in a variety of ways, for example:

- Through expansion into new markets
- Through the development of new products and services
- Through introducing increased efficiency
- Through liquidating non-essential assets
- Through updating equipment and processes to increase profitability
- Through updated marketing strategies

Private equity firms raise investments for private equity funds, which have a finite term of seven to 10 years. This is a long-term, wealth-building strategy designed for those who are looking for a more set-it-and-forget-it approach to investing.

Specialized private equity types

Different private equity firms and funds specialize in different types of private equity, including the following:

- Distressed investing, which focuses on companies that are struggling with serious financial shortfalls
- Growth equity, which funds the scaling-up of companies following the startup phase
- Sector specialist funds, which may focus on individual types of companies including those in tech or energy
- Secondary buyouts, which focus on the sale of companies that have already been purchased by another private equity firm
- Carve-outs which focus on buying units or subsidiary companies of larger corporate entities

Whatever strategy you choose, we're confident that real estate investing offers an exceptional opportunity.

Any market, any economy, there's a real estate investment strategy that's right and workable for you.

Chapter 4

Win For Your Family in a Massive Way

We think it's important to talk about where we come from and how we got here.

Why? Because it gives you a sense of how possible it is to achieve exceptional results in your own life and it's important to see how the principles we've outlined apply in real life.

What follows are our life stories. We hope they'll help you forge your own path as you move forward and create your own exceptional outcomes!

Dani's childhood story

Where you end up in life has a lot to do with where you started and how you grew up. So I think where I want to start is, Number One, I grew up in a very positive environment.

It was always, "You can do anything that you want. You are fantastic. You're amazing. What do you want to do? We support you."

There was never anything that I could not try with

absolute confidence because I was allowed to try and my parents were telling me I was going to be great at it if I tried it. So that's probably why I've tried so many things and have never been afraid to do something new and just tackle something.

I've always been very money-motivated and some people would say, you know, that's evil. But the reason behind my desire for money was because I grew up poor—or at least that's how I perceived it.

We lived in nice houses, not like the house we have now, just a regular house. We were always taken care of. We did move a lot. But we never had enough money to do whatever we wanted or take vacations or buy the really cool things that all of our friends were buying. So I always viewed our family at that stage of life as poor because I saw other people doing more than we could.

My parents were not money-motivated. They were very much, what I would call, "giving-back moti-vated." They were children's ministers and we went to church three times a week. They directed a youth choir that traveled and did ministry and mission trips. I remember being on buses and doing work for the church. That was their motivation and a big part of the focus of our upbringing was on giving back and helping others.

It was a combination of their positivity and the desire to take care of them because of how much they have given of themselves that has motivated me over the years. I thought, Number One, I don't ever want to want for money. I want to be able to take care of us and be able to take care of my family. In addition, I want to give back because my parents taught me that giving back was a good thing.

So if I had all the money in the world, those three things are the things I'd like to achieve. Taking care of myself, taking care of my family, and giving back: Those were my motivations to chase money, and the fulfillment was to make sure that I was achieving those things. It wasn't about money as an object. It was about money and the impact it could have and the ability it could give me to do so much more.

Flip's childhood story

So just take Dani's story and remove her and insert me. Were we poor? No, we weren't poor, but we definitely weren't wealthy. We had a nice house, but we didn't have the same things as the other kids. When they were wearing Jordache jeans, I was wearing Huskies.

Shoes were the big thing: When everyone was wearing Reebok and K-Swiss, I wore Keds. It was brutal. I was so motivated, even back then, when I was 10 years old, I wanted a pair of Vans. If you don't remember Vans, just Google them. They were super popular back then and they're even more popular now.

I wanted the black and white checkerboard Vans, and I wanted them so badly. They cost $30 in 1980. So I saved up every penny I could for I don't know how long. Those were the best shoes ever. I've probably got six or seven pairs of Vans now, and it goes back to childhood.

I grew up in the church as well. My dad was a Lutheran pastor. My mom taught Sunday School and directed the choir. My dad passed away when I was growing up so my mom took care of me while she was a principal and director of a Christian day school.

I was always involved in the church. In fact, Dani and I compared notes on our younger years and who was more involved or who went to the most services in one day. I won the 'most services' because on Easter Sunday 1980, I racked up five services in one day from 6 am to 4:30 pm! Just like hers, it was a very positive environment to grow up in. I think that's why I always knew I could accomplish whatever I wanted.

College and cruise ships: Dani's story

I was playing trumpet, and I auditioned for a scholarship, receiving a full ride to Southeastern University. Back then, it was called Southeastern Bible College. My major was music performance because I loved playing the trumpet, I knew I was good at it, and I knew I didn't want to teach.

Even though I didn't end up as a professional musician long-term, I wouldn't say that college was a waste for me. It was a good experience and you learn a lot of life lessons while you're in college. After graduating, I became a music minister, which was a natural progression after the way that I grew up as a child of ministers.

Ultimately, however, I decided that this was not my career, not my future. This was not something that I was passionate about, even though I was good at it.

When I was in college, I auditioned and was accepted to the Christmas Brass performance group at Walt Disney World. I loved the performance aspect and played in the parks for three years. Because of the connections I still had there, I ended up being invited to go on Carnival Cruise Line ships to work. I thought that sounded interesting and fun. I was still young and that sounded like a better fit for me.

Flip's story

So when it came time to choose a college, there wasn't much choice for me since my whole family went to Michigan State. As a freshman, my major was computer science, but I took my trumpet because I loved playing in all kinds of bands. I auditioned for the 300 + member Spartan Marching Band before school had even started.

A few weeks prior to my audition, the director pulled me aside and said, "Hey, I'm not sure that trumpet is the right section for you, I would like you to audition for a different section." So that was the kick in the pants I needed; I practiced so hard that summer and got into the Michigan State marching band, auditioning before classes started that fall.

I ended up getting first chair out of 72 trumpets and the director never said another word!

After that I thought, "I really enjoy doing this and I

might be kind of good at it as well." So I transitioned out of my computer science major and started to focus on playing more music.

I stayed at Michigan State for almost five years, majoring in music performance and music education. Subsequently, I transferred to Western Michigan with a full-ride scholarship to continue my studies.

That winter of 1997 was so cold my car door froze open and I was ready for a change of scenery. A friend of mine called me from Jacksonville, Florida saying, "You need to come down here. I've got an extra room." And so I auditioned for the University of North Florida in Jacksonville and received a full ride. College number three, for those of you keeping score at home, and still no degree.

The first week or so at school in Jacksonville, everyone's saying, "You need to go audition for Disney. They've got this great winter program called Christmas Brass."

I auditioned and was accepted. At the first rehearsal, a phenomenal trumpet player was sitting next to me. He said, "Oh, you go to North Florida. Do you know Danielle?" That's how I first heard of Dani. The year she left the group was the year I started.

Four or five months later, another friend called and said, "Hey, I need a lead trumpet player on a cruise ship." It was Monday and I had to be onboard on Friday. I loaded up the car and headed to Miami.

I got on the cruise ship and the very first night, the

trumpet player next to me said, "Oh, you went to North Florida, you played Disney, so you must know Danielle." I thought, "That's it! I have to meet this Danielle person!!"

Another year and a half passed, and a hurricane came to the Caribbean. A number of cruise ships diverted course from the hurricane and were docked at the Port of Nassau all at one time.

The cruise ship I was on had a cocktail set with old 40s and 50s dance music for the Captain. We had our tuxedos on and we were playing Glen Miller and the trumpet player said, "Hey, remember Danielle that I was telling you about? That's her in the front row."

Now I am thinking, "Finally! I get to meet this person!" So we played the whole hour and the curtain went down. I went through the curtain to look for her and she was gone. She had come over with her band to hear us play and they left as soon as we finished.

I hurried and got down to the gangway and off to the pier. It was about 6 pm and I was running down the pier in 100-degree weather with 100 percent humidity in a full tuxedo yelling her name. I've been following her for so long, I know all about her, I've heard all the stories. Never once thinking She has no idea who I am.

And so she turns around thinking Who the heck is this guy? So that is literally how we met. Then her band and my band went out that night and hung out all night and, I'm sure, got into loads of trouble.

Just a few months later, we both got moved over to the Carnival Destiny. We played for a couple more years, and it was halfway through the year 2000. We were working with the art auctioneer on board and when Dani found out how much auctioneers make, she threw open my cabin door, pointed right at me, and declared, "You're going to be an art auctioneer."

We both retired as professional musicians, put down our trumpets, and became art auctioneers. With this new position, we got to go on a lot of other different cruise lines. Norwegian, Royal Caribbean, Celebrity, Crystal, Holland America. We got to travel and see a lot more of the world.

That led to us moving on land and traveling to different cities all across the United States conducting art auctions in hotel ballrooms. When 2008 hit, it not only affected the real estate market, it affected all of the markets. Being someone who was selling decorative pieces of artwork didn't entice people at that point, especially when many were losing their homes.

Falling in love... with real estate

Dani: So as the art auction gig was winding down, I was trying to figure out what I could transition into so that I could help Flip transition out of art auctions as well.

I looked into life insurance, financial planning, mutual funds and mortgage: but I really didn't love any of them.

Finally, it was at the beginning of 2008 that we got to the point where we were trying real estate. Boom. I fell in love.

We both became Realtors but what we didn't have was a network. We had been on cruise ships and traveling every single weekend.

It took us eight months to get our first deal done as Realtors because we just didn't know anyone. It was horrible. It was just Un-Fun. We realized very quickly that we were at the mercy of the people we were working with, including unreasonable sellers and buyers who wanted you to jump at a moment's notice. We didn't want to live a life like that.

We decided to be investors instead. That was kind of a passion of mine anyway, so when I was looking at different possibilities for what we'd do next, real estate investing was something I wanted to learn more about.

We reached out to three different mentors. We emailed different people in the local area because we wanted to learn from somebody who was local. Only one person replied to us and it was Phill Grove. He is someone who's been coaching and teaching very successfully for a very long time, and who taught us 12 different ways to buy and sell real estate. We went to a two-day class and ended up forming a team with our broker and her husband and then another colleague. So we all went on this journey together.

Flip and I have always been of the mindset that we

never wanted to do things by ourselves. We like to work with other people because we learn faster. We keep each other motivated and accountable. So we started our journey into real estate investing as a team.

We started doing mortgage assignments and short sales, primarily.

We printed our message on bright neon color paper and we targeted neighborhoods where we wanted to get houses. It was a grand adventure and we learned so much. Most importantly, we learned how to adjust our marketing and our strategies very quickly depending on the market. I think that's probably been the most valuable lesson from our career.

We believe everything happens for a reason. We chose real estate in a down market, took advantage of it, and launched our careers.

We became known as the REI Rockstars during that time because we were so successful in what we were doing. Our coach said that less than 10 percent of the people that he coaches are successful at that level, so it's not just because of him, we were action-takers.

And when you're a coach, you see the same thing. People don't do what you tell them to do. We did exactly what our coach told us to do and look at what we were able to accomplish.

Flip: Going back to the reams of bright paper, we didn't write on them. We wrote on one piece of paper and photocopied it 500 times. Then we would wake up and go out in the morning—because it's Texas, you have to go out in the morning when it's not as hot—and that's also when people have typically left their house already. Then they would see this colored paper on their door when they came home from work.

We were out one morning and I was walking down one side of the street and Dani was walking down the other. All of a sudden, I saw a woman in her driveway, and she came up to Dani and barked at her saying, "What are you putting on these doors?" That lady was not happy at all.

Dani didn't skip a beat and quickly replied, "We're on a raising [home] values campaign and we're looking for houses to buy in this neighborhood so that we can help raise the value of everyone else's houses."

This lady went from grumpy to happy in a snap! She gave us the lowdown on everybody in the neighborhood: "Well, that guy over there, and make sure you talk to this person here...." We still laugh about that morning and the "Raising Values Campaign". I always joke about writing that on my arm so I would never forget that line...it was brilliant!

We were working on a shoestring budget, so we did as much as we possibly could without spending hardly any money. And we did that for years because we had burned through most of our savings in those 8-12 months when we were Realtors.

It was a great learning experience. It taught us how to be a chameleon and try different strategies. So from there, we decided to teach others what we were doing and we became coaches. We also partnered with an attorney and started doing 'Subject to-Wrap' strategies as well as continuing to do mortgage assignments and short sales.

Understanding how to navigate and shift and adapt is really important. It's something that we talk about a lot. When you are working with others or learning from others, find out if they understand the micro cycles and strategies that work at different times so that you can shift and adapt.

In 2015, while living in Arizona, we started to work with an investor in Ohio. He was doing a strategy that we had not heard of before called Turnkey Real Estate. We quickly realized how much we liked this strategy and we started partnering to sell turnkey real estate deals. I found myself walking around in my backyard in Arizona talking to a guy in New Hampshire about a house in Ohio that neither of us had ever been to in person. It was all about the numbers. We realized that we could do a lot more of this if we lived in Ohio so we packed up and moved there in 2015. From there, we fell in love with this strategy; it's an investing model that helps you build wealth. You partner with high-net-worth individuals like doctors, lawyers and entrepreneurs who understand the power of wealth-building through real estate but don't have the time to do it themselves.

Using a resource like us to be able to buy the properties and have it completely handled for them was something that appealed to them. It allowed us to help other people on their wealth-building journey, too.

So in 2017, we created Freedom Real Estate Group. It was just Dani and I, working out of our house in Ohio. The main reason we started it is because deals just kept coming to us and we knew it was going to continue to grow. We just didn't know how FAST it was going to grow.

We knew that we couldn't do it all by ourselves so we added leverage by making our first hire, Betty, who is still the heart and soul of Freedom Real Estate Group to this day. The three of us were working out of our dining room so I started to search for an office. A month later we got our first office that had room for growth. It was a 5000 square foot office for just the three of us. We could have played touch football and not touched anyone.

From there, it just snowballed, big time. We needed our own renovation company, so we started Bulldog Renovations. We needed our own property management company, so we started Independence Property Management. Everything was born out of necessity— when we needed something, we created a company to do it. Next thing you know, we completely filled that office space and had people working in the hallways.

Dani: I think that's the important part of the story: If you're a turnkey operator and you're doing things in service to other high net worth individuals, there are many pieces to the puzzle. Renovation was our first pain point. We had times when contractors weren't doing what they were supposed to be doing—they were taking pictures of completed work that wasn't completed. So out of necessity, we had to build Bulldog Renovations so that we could control everything in-house and control the product we were putting out.

With property management, we tried outsourcing to five different companies, and it was terrible. And I'm not telling you that we're perfect because I always tell people we are human like anybody else. But we had to build a company to handle things the way we needed them handled.

Flip: From the very beginning, I was the acquisitions department and the majority of the deals that we got, like 99.999 percent, were from wholesalers. So I had quite a network of wholesalers and I was always following up with them and getting deals to make the business run. Then all of a sudden, that well dried up and we said, Oh, this can't happen. We need to be in control of this ourselves.

Thus, the fifth company, Cash for Ohio Houses, came about, an acquisitions company designed to constantly bring in leads.

Dani: And now we're even on TV. And those five companies are the core of what we wanted to build and sustain.

It wasn't a perfect road and we made a lot of mistakes. It was a rollercoaster. The road to success is not a straight line, but you grow a lot by pushing through and learning from your failures. That's what makes you more intelligent in terms of what you should be doing and how you should be handling projects, leading your team, making decisions, and choosing your markets. You learn by doing.

Our process has always been to dig in and not be afraid of making mistakes. We understood that sometimes we would lose money, but through the process, we knew that we would eventually be able to say, "Okay, well now we know how to do this".

We call our companies the Freedom Family of Companies. Vertical integration allows you to control all the pieces of the puzzle. It's not perfect but we get better every day and that's the goal.

There are always hurdles in real estate. There's always a new situation, a new regulation, even something that you'll say "Whoa, that broke in the house, and what is that exactly?" Because that's never happened before.

I'm grateful for the team that we've been able to put together and the people who are in place leading those five companies.

Moving into multi-family

So there came a point in our real estate career as we were building our companies when we had a package deal come our way, and it was 15 properties. Twelve of them were single family, and three of them were duplexes.

This package also came with a 56-unit apartment complex. This particular seller did not want to break up the package even though we just wanted the 15 properties for our turnkey business. When we are looking for deals, we love buying packages because there's very little competition.

Since the seller did not want to sell the 56-unit multi-family apart from the other properties, we decided we were going to wholesale them to another investor because we weren't into apartment investing yet. I always wanted to get into apartments, but that was a little bit down the road because we already had our hands full building five companies.

Keep in mind, on top of everything else, this was 2020, so COVID was just starting when we got this deal. We found a buyer for the apartments but the lender fell out so we had to find another lender which extended the contract. This process ended up taking so long that both us and the seller were frustrated and the seller was ready to back out of the deal completely so we told the buyer we couldn't wait any longer and we had to get the deal closed.

The buyer was willing to close but he wanted to

change the terms of the deal, so we said, "Forget it. We'll buy it." Fortunately, we have a great network and one of the investors in our mastermind had over 2,000 apartment units in their portfolio so we asked them if they would partner with us and they said yes.

It took us two weeks to do all of the inspections and put together the money to buy it. It was a $1.3 million purchase with an $800,000 rehab. It was pretty much all occupied except for one unit. October 15, 2020, after a rush of activity to complete all our due diligence we closed on our biggest deal to date and were proud owners of a 56-unit apartment complex that we later nicknamed "Drugs, Thugs & Bugs".

After 14 months of unending issues and stories that will be told for years to come, we finally had the property stabilized. By month 21 we got final approval on our refinance. When the refinance was complete, we looked back at our projected numbers to compare them to the actual numbers and realized the deal was a home run, slam dunk. What we found funny was that while we were in the middle of the storm experiencing every possible nightmare at this property, it never occurred to us how much money we would make when it was finally done. It definitely prepared us for the multi-family world and made us feel like we can do any deal at this point.

We never ended up reaching out to our partners through all this chaos because we didn't want to worry them. We knew we could push through any issues that came at us. But when we told our partners about it afterward, she said, "I can't believe you went through all of that and just took it in stride!" But for us, having done so many turnkey rehabs, this just felt the same, except on a larger scale.

With any project, no matter the size, every single day you're just problem-solving. Instead of getting overwhelmed by the number of problems or the scope of the project, just focus on one challenge at a time, solve it, then move on to the next.

Despite all of the challenges, once you see the income coming in and the stabilization of the property, you start to see there are so many economies of scale in terms of the cost of contractors, because:

- They are all in one spot.
- They can order in bulk and put everything into one of the units.
- They don't have to travel to multiple job sites.
- They can rehab multiple units at the same time.
- There were only four buildings instead of 56 buildings.

We learned so much through this experience. As we got close to the end of it and saw the money starting to come in, we said excitedly, "we should do more of this". It was really exciting to be thrown into the experience. When it comes down to it, we found out we're very comfortable being uncomfortable and there are three key takeaways that have always helped us:

1 - The road to success is never a straight line; you

grow a lot by pushing through and learning from your failures. You're problem-solving every day with any project, no matter the size. Instead of getting overwhelmed by the number of problems or the scope of the project, just focus on one challenge at a time, solve it, then move on to the next.

2 - The fastest way to success is through finding others already on your path who have seen the results you're looking to achieve. Throughout our life and growing number of companies, we have always sought out wisdom from those who were where we wanted to be.

3 - From the raising values campaign to the multiple businesses we've built today, it all stems from a quote we love from Zig Ziglar: "You can have everything in life you want, if you will just help enough other people get what they want."

Epilogue

Find Your Freedom

Freedom Family Investments is designed to provide high-net-worth investors with the opportunity to go on their own journey to freedom through passive income.

As we were developing our companies and our investment portfolio, we were thinking of different ways to offer options to investors who want to come along on this ride with us. That's really where our passion is— ensuring that our family and team are taken care of and helping our investors do everything we're doing. We want to be able to do this full-time and continue to give back to the professional community that we're part of.

Giving back is such a core belief for us as a family of companies. We do it now, but imagine what we could all do as we continue to build passive income opportunities. We can give money to causes that we care about.

As a high-net-worth investor, you've worked hard for your money. It's time to transition some of that active income—the kind you're constantly working for and tending to—to passive income.

If you want to build wealth through real estate, and you are a doctor or are in another high-earning, high-net-worth career that you're passionate about and that you love, you have to find an expert in the space where you want to invest so that you can build that wealth and live the life that you want, that you deserve, so that you can do things on your terms. That's what Freedom Family Investments is designed to help you do.

We offer a variety of options, whether you're looking for a hands-on approach or a totally passive approach to real estate investing. You can find more information at Freedom Family Investments (FreedomFamily.Investments) and make an appointment to speak with us and determine which path makes the most sense for your bandwidth and your goals.

About The Authors

Flip and Dani Lynn Robison are the co-founders of Freedom Family Investments and the Freedom Family of Companies, a collection of real estate businesses headquarted in Centerville, Ohio, with over 50 team members and growing. They have bought and sold over 1,200 properties and have ownership in over 600 multi-family units. As realtors in 2008, they quickly realized that real estate investing was where they needed to be.

Famed for their very first 56-unit apartment complex nicknamed "Drugs, Thugs & Bugs", you can hear the horror stories and lessons at events and on podcasts nationwide. Everything that could go wrong did, but grit and perseverance won the day, and the reward was over $2 Million dollars in profit in 21 months. Flip and Dani have been featured at speaking events and enjoy appearing on podcasts to educate and inspire others to pursue their freedom through real estate.

Flip and Dani have an interesting history. They both went to college in Florida, both played trumpet professionally at Walt Disney World in Ohio and on Carnival Cruise Lines. Yet their paths first crossed when a hurricane hit the Carribean, causing both of their cruise ships to dock in Nassau, Bahamas at the same exact time. They enjoyed over a decade of life at sea, and they are now happy to be living on terra firma, parents to two feisty bulldogs named Spartacus and Rosie and one golden retriever named Bailey.

The Robisons find great fulfillment helping others discover their own freedom strategy. Reach out to start building your freedom portfolio. Together they are hosts of "The Freedom Show", where listeners can tune in for free financial education and real estate investor culture.

How to Connect:

+ 1 (884) 877-0888
invest@freedomfamilyinvestments.com

+ 1 (844) 877-0888
1st Edition oops!
LI

The *Freedom* Show

More Real Estate Education

Tune into "The Freedom Show" on YouTube and on your favorite podcasting app. Learn about real estate investing, real opportunities and investor culture.

https://freedomfamilyinvestments.com/show

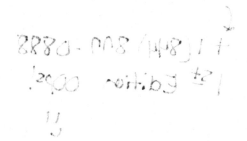

Free Audiobook

Included with this hardcopy is a complimentary audio version. Experience the book in a whole new way, read by the authors themselves.

https://freedomfamilyinvestments.com/audiobook
Your Password is: Keepitreal

Download the audiobook using the QR code or by typing in the URL, it's free.

NOTES

NOTES

NOTES

NOTES

Made in the USA
Monee, IL
26 May 2023

34076603R00056